DEAR JAMES AND TYRA

ENJOY THE JOURNEY
LIVE THE DREAM
EXPLORE YOUR WORLD
KEEP IT GREEN

A BETTER BROTHER I COULD NEVER HAVE WISHED FOR!

THANKS FOR BEING WITH ME

WITH LOVE

Around the World in 80 Poems

Rhyming Reasons to Travel the Globe...Or Not!

Graham Relton

authorHOUSE®

AuthorHouse™ UK Ltd.
500 Avebury Boulevard
Central Milton Keynes, MK9 2BE
www.authorhouse.co.uk
Phone: 08001974150

© 2007 Graham Relton. All rights reserved.

No part of this book may be reproduced, stored in a retrieval system, or transmitted by any means without the written permission of the author.

First published by AuthorHouse 10/30/2007

ISBN: 978-1-4343-3276-9 (sc)

Printed in the United States of America
Bloomington, Indiana

This book is printed on acid-free paper.

"I'm going travelling whether you come with me or not!" Without this ultimatum from my then girlfriend and now wife I may never have taken the plunge to step off the career ladder and take a year off to circumnavigate the globe.

To my gorgeous wife Keira,
this book is for you.
Thank you.

A trip of a lifetime
Nervous and excited, it's so hard to express
What the future has in store is more happiness
So much to look forward to, so much to see and do
A new journey starts soon, a dream come true
Stepping off the rat race to face the unknown
A test of each other to see how much we've grown
A lot to leave behind…routine, family and friends
But lots to discover, new people, cultures, trends?
Creating memories for eternity, sights, smells and sounds
It won't always be easy; we'll have our ups and downs
Going round the world together, we'll see it through
But my trip of a lifetime began when I met you!

Foreword

Travel, I have found is an eye opener, a gift to the fortunate ones in the world who have sufficient health and money to explore new destinations as a matter of choice rather than necessity. I realised that I was one of the lucky ones to have an opportunity to taste the adventure, to see and experience some of the rich cultural journeys and many natural and manmade wonders that the world has to offer. It didn't take me long to appreciate what I have and I soon gained a greater understanding of just how lucky I was to be born in the UK. My perception of poverty, disability and freedom was challenged in many places. I guess what I am saying is that when we travel we have a responsibility, both socially and environmentally, we should

> 'Take home memories and photographs but leave only footprints.'
> *- Chief Seattle*

Each and every one of us leaves their footprint on the world. My partner and I tried to minimise and reduce our footprint: Where possible, we travelled by train or bus, we offset our carbon emissions, planted native plants, supported local people, businesses and good causes, respected traditions and customs and cleaned up after ourselves.

> 'You must be the change you wish to see in the world.'
> *- Mahatma Gandhi*

Graham Relton

10% of the author's profits will be donated to environmental charities.

Contents

Foreword

Introduction

Mexico
    1. Hola

Creepy Doll Museum, Mexico

    2. Police stations and hospitals
    3. Tree hugger
    4. Pop culture

USA
    5. Super power?
    6. Neighbours
    7. Remember
    8. Star wars

9. Less Bush
10. Rocky road
11. Supersize
12. Quizza
13. Lake or sea?
14. State fate
15. Soccer shocker
16. Mor' than a man can handle
17. Road trip
18. It's gonna blow!
19. Pride

Odd one out, USA

20. The 'Rock'
21. L.Aliens

Fiji
> 22. We have all the time in the world…
> 23. Motherland
> 24. Numb-tea

New Zealand
> 25. Lamb love
> 26. Hot Water Beach
> 27. Sweet as…

G-force, New Zealand

> 28. On the brink
> 29. Counselling needed?

Australia
> 30. Pommie-bashing
> 31. Walking a fine line
> 32. Spellbinding
> 33. Sydney splat!
> 34. Baha'i

35. Crikey!
36. Sand 'man'
37. Bush tucker

Caution: Cassowary, Australia

38. Good 'greef'

Bali

39. Gurgling
40. Millionaires
41. Spectacular, spectacular
42. Shelve it
43. Careful where you tread

Singapore
- 44. Nutcracker sling
- 45. Spice of life
- 46. Cold rush, hot flush

Malaysia
- 47. Twins

Twin towers, Malaysia

- 48. Masochistic
- 49. Rubber

Thailand
    50. Muay Thai
    51. Did the earth move for you?
    52. King
    53. Shit happens
    54. School-tide

Laos
    55. Slow boat

Barbecued rat anyone? Laos

Cambodia
    56. Angkor what?
    57. Crown jewels

Vietnam
   58. Leap of faith

Green Cross Code, Vietnam

   59. Play the game
   60. Greasy Chopstick
   61. Splash act
   62. Tortured by the beast
   63. Dirty laundry

Hong Kong
   64. Happy Valley
   65. Hong Kong wrong
   66. Fragrant Harbour

China
   67. Stand out
   68. Split pants

69. Travel wall

Valentine's Day, China

70. The Chairman
71. New Olympic event
72. Quiet please!

Mongolia
73. Law of the sod
74. Rightful ruler
75. You can leave your hat on?

Russia
- 76. Red tape
- 77. Have faith
- 78. Grin and share it?

Final Thoughts
- 79. Final destination?
- 80. Travel Charades

Introduction

345 days, 16 countries, 4 continents, 3 hospitals, 2 wedding rings, 1 police station and a day lost forever.

"You must have seen the whole world."

This is what people say to my wife and I when we tell them that we took the plunge and left our comfortable jobs to circumnavigate the globe for the best part of year. Well the world is a pretty big place and you would need quite a few life times to see every corner of it. There is only so much you can see and do in 345 days, only so many temples you can visit, only so many grotty hostels you can stay in, only so many new foods you can taste, only so many people you can meet and only so many things you can remember…I think you get the picture. I started writing poems in the first week in a hostel in the heart of Mexico City as a way of documenting the once in a lifetime trip we had embarked on and I carried on until the last leg of our epic journey on the Trans-Siberian Express across China and Mongolia to Russia. Our circumnavigation of the world took us from the pyramids in Mexico to the supersized U.S. of A., a secret wedding in Fiji, 'Zorbing' in New Zealand and some 'Pommie-bashing' in Australia. We became rich in Bali, spoilt in Singapore and amazed in Malaysia. Survived an earthquake and a colonoscopy in Thailand, dashed across to Laos, were overwhelmed by the temples in Cambodia and played 'chicken' with the bikes in Vietnam. Blinded by the lights in Hong Kong, dodged the phlegm in China, took our hats off to Mongolia and finally cut through the red tape to reach our final destination of Russia.

This book is a collection of my individual observations, my ups and my downs, the serious and the funny. I hope it inspires, amuses and questions you the reader, giving you rhyming reasons to travel the globe…or not!

1. Hola

Despite what they say Mexico City is not all bad
Once through the smog there is a lot to be had
The airport taxi ride certainly opened our eyes
Red lights, kids in bins, was this really wise?
The pyramids at Teotihuacan towered above our little 'bods'
The Aztecs named them 'the place where men become Gods'
The Floating Gardens, the yearly Festival of the Spring
Many boats, many Mexicans with a picnic they did bring
If you ever plan to visit, a little jaunt for the hols
Something you should not miss, is the Museum of the Dolls
A scarier, creepier, freakier place you will not see
Full of maimed and limbless dolls…Not everyone's 'cup of tea'
Passed by the Plaza Garibaldi where the Mariachis stay
Like prostitutes they wait until a customer will pay
The markets were electric, you really would concur
A local delicacy on offer, try fried grasshopper
It tasted kind of strange, most refuse to have a lick
A bit like crunchy chicken with a seafood kick
So with twenty-five million people and a reputation as a dive
I'd like to beg to differ…we came out alive!

2. Police stations and hospitals

Police stations and hospitals
They weren't part of the plan
We should have been exploring
Or working on our tan
A lost purse and food poisoning
It's just the end of week two
Get all the bad stuff out of the way
I think that's what we'll do

3. Tree hugger

That species of cypress
In Tule it stands guard
It cannot fail to impress
In the little churchyard
At fifty-eight metres around
It stands majestic, so high
Rooted to the ground
But reaching to the sky
At over two thousand years old
I'd like to have heard a few
Of the stories it could have told
And if only it knew?
The locals believe it's sacred
It brings them to their knees
As it looms overhead
One of God's oldest trees
And if you stare a little while
In the bark they appear
You may spot a crocodile
A lion or a deer
It's a paradise for the birds
In nests that keep them snug
It's hard to put into words
I just wanted to give it a hug

4. Pop culture

The Indian people of Chamula
Say "Kushee" instead of "Hola"
And like many other people
They worship Coca-cola
It's part of their culture
From the workers to the Chief
More than a fizzy pop
Rather a religious belief
In the colours of the corn,
From cans and bottles they slurp
The evil spirits are released
When they belch or burp!

5. Super power?

The Constitution of the United States
Seven articles with many a section
A bill of rights with lots of amendments
A British system in reflection
With similar laws and similar ways
But with a President at the throne?
Stealing all the British ideas
Passing them off as their own
Today, U.S. citizens should worry
With a government who've made it clear
Stripping away privacy and freedom
Controlling them all with fear

6. Neighbours

Connie Picciotto is passionate
To get the job done
She's been protesting outside the White House,
Since 1981

Ignored, beaten and arrested
Regrets, you will not find
Just a simple message
Peace, freedom and justice for mankind

7. Remember

A poignant memorial
Freedom to roam
Honour the men and women
Who didn't make it home
Black polished granite
Listed chronologically
Thousands reflected
Sacrificed tragically
Remember Vietnam
Let the candle burn
Such a waste of life
Will they ever learn?

8. Star wars

Arlington National Cemetery
Hundreds of thousands do rest
Human struggle and sacrifice
They've taken the ultimate test
Many classes, creeds and races
From the JFK eternal flame
To the tomb of the unknowns
Where do we lay the blame?
All have answered their country's call
Unimaginable horrors they saw
But you have to ask the question
Does this country really need war?

9. Less Bush

The U.S. administration
Is ignoring all the facts
More focused on the oil
And whom they will attack
Well global warming is real
No more 'hush-hush'
Let's start to make a difference
More trees and less Bush

10. Rocky road

The Philadelphia Art Museum is so popular
Not just for the artworks inside
People visit from all over the world
For a ticket on a nostalgia ride
Jostling for space for a photo
Secretly the theme tune they hum
To re-live the 'Rocky' experience
Shadow boxing up the steps they run

11. Supersize

Stuck on every corner
Fast food joints
"Make it big" or "Supersize"

Everywhere you look
Jiggling and wobbling
Fat bellies and fat thighs

On the sidewalk
On the subway
Every day and every hour

Just look at us
We're big and fat
We are the superpower

So if you're on a diet
With your weight
You do grapple

Make yourself feel slimmer
Why don't you
Visit the Big Apple!

12. Quizza

Traditional Chicago pizza
Have you ever tried a piece?
It's a strange combination
Of a pizza and a quiche

13. Lake or sea?

When is a lake a lake?
When does it become a sea?
Lake Michigan is so vast
It looks like a sea to me
One of America's great lakes
But how can it really be?
I couldn't see the other side
It looks like a sea to me
If the lake is actually a lake
Then why is it seagulls I see?
Shouldn't they call them 'lakegulls'?
It looks like a sea to me

14. State fate

We took our first Amtrak
Across the U.S. of A.
It's better than flying
In almost every way
It may not be quicker
And many people 'slam it'
but it's easier on the pocket
And better for the planet
Chicago to San Francisco
With so much in between
On the 'California Zephyr'
Sights that must be seen
Traversing seven states
A camera a 'must' companion
The Mississippi river
And many a beautiful canyon
Winding through the Rockies
Small stations and big places
A real taste of America
Etched upon the faces
Comfy seats, friendly service
But not always on time
Things would be much different
If they didn't share a line
So despite the lengthy delays
Caused by Union Pacific
It didn't get us down, 'cos
We think Amtrak is terrific!

15. Soccer shocker

The U.S. World Cup coverage
Really was a shocker...
They just don't get 'real' football
Instead they call it soccer
When someone makes a tackle
That ends up out of play
They say it's 'batted out'
Show me the 'bat' I say!
The worst was a guy called 'Balboa'
A commentator I'd like to slam
He said the world's most popular player
Was the famous 'Michael' Beckham
I think that says it all
It certainly confirms my theories
When teams only from the U.S.
Can compete in the 'World' Series

16. Mor' than a man can handle

I thought about becoming a Mormon
I like the idea of more than one wife
More fun in the bedroom department
Now that sounds like the life!
But then again I'm not sure
More nagging? More work? More strife?

17. Road trip

Hire cars have a mind of their own
They don't like you to leave their city
They'd rather drive you round and round
A concrete jungle they find so pretty
Just when you find the road out of town
And for it, you make a dash
An unfamiliar warning will sound
A distracting light will flash
Buttons, switches, knobs and dials
How to turn off the back wiper?
Of the vehicle, you have no control
Like a child behind the pied piper
Finally on the 'wrong' side of the road
I escaped but still had my doubts
On a road trip through the United States
At least there's no roundabouts!

18. It's gonna blow!

Canyons, rivers, lakes
Forests, plains and hills
It couldn't be recreated
With million dollar bills
An active super volcano
A thermal wonderland
On a restless magna chamber
Geologists aim to understand
Warning, unpredictable
Geysers and mud pools
Simmering under the surface
Mother Nature's tools
Fumaroles, hot springs, toxic gases
Wild bison, elk and deer
Eagles soaring overhead
But it's the grizzlies you should fear!
Just Yogi on the picnic prowl
In Yellowstone Park, his pad
Perhaps the most beautiful park
The world has ever had?
But how much longer will it be
Thirty thousand years overdue
Mini earthquakes all the time
Hundreds, not a few
So visit soon if you choose
Because you never know
Might not be there much longer
Any minute it could blow!

19. Pride

The San Francisco Pride parade
Was fun to say the least
A cocktail of outrageousness
From the beauty to the beast
A colourful spectacle of joy
Crazy costumes all the rage
Liberating but bizarre
Friendship centre stage
Proud to celebrate themselves
That's what it's all about
What an amazing experience
Even as the odd one out

20. The 'Rock'

In the heart of San Francisco Bay
Sits an island in the mist
Surrounded by mysterious legend
Lost in the fog of its myths
In Alcatraz, the prison
The infamous they did lock
A symbol of America's dark side
A place they call the 'Rock'

21. L.Aliens

LA is all about the money
And if your face fits
Packed with plastic surgeons
Who can modify your bits.
Almost everyone we spoke with
Including the tourists too
Urgently needed treatment...
To say 'please' and 'thank you'.
Shallow, ignorant and rude
Driving round in flashy cars
In need of personality transplants
All blinded by the stars?
So let me just recap
LA is all about the wealth
I wouldn't stay too long
It's really bad for your health!

22. We have all the time in the world…

Fiji has a special time zone
A whole lot different from mine
Everything takes much longer
Clocks are set to 'Fiji time'
Don't expect anything fast
It all takes a little while
Sit back, go with the flow
It always comes with a smile

23. Motherland

As British folk, we didn't expect
The friendly welcome we received
After all the 'Empire' stole the place
So we were really quite relieved
They let us in with open arms
It's difficult to understand
Like afternoon tea with the Queen
Guests from the 'Motherland'
They thanked us for their history
We were treated like a brother
Before, they said they were cannibals
But now they don't eat each other!

24. Numb-tea

The friendly people of Fiji
Drink kava, like the Brits drink tea
To welcome you into their home
But with more pomp and ceremony
Made from the root of the yaqona
And served in a special bowl
Shout 'Bula' and clap three times
And wash it down your hole
A warning, it tastes unpleasant
But I recommend you try some
As it contains a mild narcotic
That will make your tongue go numb
So even though it looks disgusting
Nature may have found the answer
The Uni' of Aberdeen have proven
Kava's good for two types of cancer

25. Lamb love

You just can't help but notice
In the fields roaming free
One of New Zealand's biggest exports
As far as the eye can see
Like white polka dots on green
Fluffy clouds under the sun
The sheep outnumber people
By thirty-five to one
So I guess it's no surprise
As all those sheep need tagging
That one of their favourite pastimes...
...is eating lots of lamb!

26. Hot Water Beach

Hot Water Beach
Was really surreal
Rain on the brolly
Cold to the feel
With shovel in hand
We had to laugh
Dug a hole in the sand
And took a hot bath

27. Sweet as…

Do you like the idea of a skydive
But dismiss it as insane?
Have a go at extreme freefall
A skydive without the plane
Feel the G-force as you fly
Above the wind like plasticine
Look at the photos after
To see where your face has just been!

28. On the brink

It exists only in New Zealand
An icon to a nation
A fascinating evolution
Due to their geographic isolation
The kiwi was doing just fine
Surviving millions of years
Until man and his predators
Brought new and impossible fears
A unique flightless bird
More Mammalian than you think
In danger of disappearing forever
A species on the brink

www.kiwiencounter.co.nz is helping the kiwi to fight back

29. Counselling needed?

After dark at Oamaru
They ride in on the waves
Waddling up the stony beach
Towards their tiny caves
But before they reach their home
They stop for a social call
The world's smallest penguin
Only thirty centimetres tall
Fascinating birds
Blue penguins are a sight
They can sleep out at sea
And hand out a nasty bite
Swim fifty kilometres a day
In search of fish to eat
Diving a thousand times
Bring home a tasty treat
And they really are quite faithful
A breeding partner for life
A happy matrimony
Penguin husband and wife
But just like us humans
Sometimes they take the bait
Can't resist temptation
An 11% divorce rate!

30. Pommie-bashing

It's up there with the cricket...
They like to hand out a thrashing
A national sport in the making
The game of Pommie-bashing!
It's best to just play along
Not take too much to heart
Because perhaps they haven't noticed
Most were Pommies in the start

31. Walking a fine line

On the south coast of Australia
Lies the Great Ocean Road
A beautiful scenic getaway
To escape from your abode
That's what a couple did do
Living life without a care
Sneaking around having fun
In an extra-marital affair
A stroll across London Bridge
A rock formation, stunning views
But unbeknown to them
They were soon to get their dues
As the nursery rhyme goes
London Bridge did fall down
A near death experience
Soon relief became a frown
They were stranded on the rock
Just the two of them no less
To be rescued by a helicopter
Watched by the nation's press!

32. Spellbinding

Aussie rules 'foot' ball
Where you get to use your hands
A magical experience
That's hard to understand
An oval ball, an oval pitch
The sport of A.F.L.
Randomness and violence
A captivating spell
No broomsticks in sight
Organised chaos abound
Wizards in their own field
Like 'quidditch' on the ground

33. Sydney splat!

Like a kangaroo or koala
Or even a crocodile
A symbol of Australia
That clearly stands out a mile
Like the Eiffel Tower, Paris
Empire State Building, New York
Modern wonder of the world
That's made people talk and talk
Expressionist modern vision
A ship at full sail
Sixteen years to complete
An architect's holy grail
It wasn't all plain sailing
Almost didn't make the dock
Over budget, overboard?
Many problems to unlock
Finally opened by the Queen
In 1973
The most recognisable building
Perhaps you'll ever see?
If you're lucky enough to visit
One of the millions every year
Dressed up, 'Night at the Opera'
A 'bravo' and a cheer
Be watchful overhead
The 'Gods' from up above
They have the best view
And to take aim they really love
It left its mark on my cousin
Unforgettable…a sudden splat
Whilst walking to the Opera House
He got shat on by a bat!

34. Baha'i

Whatever nationality or class
Race, trade or profession
Wherever in the world
Unity is their lesson
The Baha'i are unique
All faiths have a place
Manifestations of one God
But with a different face
Krishna, Moses and Buddha
Christ or Mohammed
Weaving a different message
One cloth but different thread
What a refreshing change
No religions have to fight
All equal and in harmony
One world, mankind, one light

35. Crikey!

Crikey! He's gone...
We can't believe it's true
Crocodile Hunter's left us
The Irwin Australia Zoo
A place of wonder
A place to learn
With so much wildlife
On every turn
A legacy to continue
His family do concur
A tribute to the man
The ultimate wildlife warrior

36. Sand 'man'

I visited the largest sand island
The largest in the world no less
With lakes, rainforests and shipwrecks
But it's the sand I wish to address
What is it with sand I want to know?
Swallows stuff, burns your feet through
Blows in your face and in your food
And when wet sticks like glue
Whatever you do, you can't shift the stuff
Scrubbing hard or brushing soft
But in the car or a nice clean carpet
It's guaranteed to all fall off!

37. Bush tucker

Fair dinkum, I didn't mean it
It just turned out that way
I lost my wife, it wasn't my fault
Please believe what I say
Supposed to be a bonza day
A new adrenalin rush
White water rafting adventure
With a trek first in the bush
We were separated for the first time
No worries...she's with the guide
So I thought, I was mistaken
I should have had her by my side
But come on, what's to fear?
It's only a forest we're in!
A rain forest, more like a jungle
Her patience was wearing thin
Spiders, snakes, crocodiles
And in the water a blood sucker
Prehistoric killer birds...
Was my wife to be bush tucker?
But then we heard some yelling
She found us, a face like thunder
If looks could really kill
I'd be six feet down under
She wasn't 'stoked' to see me
A smile she couldn't force
If she'd had her way that moment
I would have been divorced!

38. Good 'greef'

The Great Barrier Reef, I couldn't wait
But I couldn't wait to get back
I kept remembering the news story
Of the boat that couldn't keep track
I snorkelled a bit, enjoyed the views
All the time, the boat in sight
No need to outstay my welcome
No need to stay the night
I was included in the head count
Which really improved my mood
Don't get me wrong I loved the place
I just didn't fancy being fish food!

39. Gurgling

Like many other countries
You don't drink the water
But I think I swallowed some
I don't think I ought to
A gurgling deep inside
I was sensing something smelly
I ran in different ways
My bout of Bali belly

40. Millionaires

It's been a while since the Bali bombs
But the effects are still being felt
For every person who stays away
Another blow is dealt
It's hit the locals hard
Of this I have no doubt
But all the people who stay away
Are the ones missing out
It's as safe as any other place
Despite the evil deed
Don't be a person to stay away
Don't let the fear succeed
An island with so much to offer
Show the Balinese who cares
All you people who stay away
Come and be millionaires!

41. Spectacular, spectacular

Spectacular, spectacular
The Balinese know how to dance
Enchanting performances
Put you in a trance
Good and evil battling
Drama, chants and song
Mesmerising rituals
Characters so strong
Mythological creatures
Kings and witches you will find
Elaborate costumes
Masks to hide behind
Intricate moves, bulging eyes
Music, fire and twists
Dancing Bali style
You wouldn't want to miss

42. Shelve it

The rice fields of Bali
An attraction in themselves
Carved into the hills
A patchwork of shelves
Complex natural irrigation
The terraces are the key
Dating from the 9th century
...Man's ingenuity

43. Careful where you tread

Most of the Balinese are Hindu
But they don't put their Trinity on show
Unlike the Hindus in India
Who like to let you know
The religion is practised differently
But in temples they do pray
With vacant shrines and empty thrones
More subtle, is their way
Watch out for the small offerings
In coconut leaf, they're stood
To placate the bad spirits
And pay homage to the good
They are impossible to avoid
Everywhere you turn your head
Filled with flowers, food and incense
Just be careful where you tread

44. Nutcracker sling

Rich in colonial history
A throwback to the past
A peak into the lives
Of the upper, upper class
Old traditional fans
Wafting from the ceiling
A taste of the high life...
What a feeling
An Asian institution
Raffles is the place
An extravagant host
To many a famous face
Lounging in the luxury
Pink cocktails all round
Singapore Sling in hand
But what is that sound?
Crunching, crackling peanuts
Floor of shells like a sea
Give the Long Bar a miss
If you have nut allergies

45. Spice of life

Little India, Singapore
Truly sensual overload
A colourful thriving hub
Forefathers customs sowed
Religion, family and food
Enduring threads in their lives
Woven past and present
Traditions of old survive
A riot of jewelled saris
Deafening flower garlands
Pulsating aromatic cuisine
Henna tattoos upon the hands
Temples, arts, arcades
Knick-knacks and snacks all sold
You may chance upon a parrot
Your future it beholds
It awakens all the senses
A taste for it, occurred
Next perhaps 'Big India'?
A new wanderlust has stirred

46. Cold rush, hot flush

The humidity in Singapore
Turning your body to lead
It also turns some people
Crazy in the head!
Down by Clarke Quay
Where people like to meet
Somebody has decided
To have air-con on the street
Refreshing, maybe not
Will people ever learn?
Climate control all wrong
Too much money to burn
Warming the planet
To cool down the place
Extravagance gone mad
Such a bloody waste!

47. Twins

Malaysia's national landmark
Kuala Lumpur's face
A symbol of their growth
Industrialisation embraced
The Petronas Twin Towers
Finally had their birth
In 1996
The tallest twins on earth
A portal to the sky
Clad in stainless steel
Socio-economic giants
A reflection of their zeal
They are not just futuristic
Concrete, steel and glass
They encompass Islamic principles
Foundations in the past
Geometric, eight-pointed stars
Each structure's floor plan
Five tiers atop the towers
The 'five pillars' of Islam
Unity within unity
Stability and rationality
Harmony of the form
Incorporated architecturally

48. Masochistic

The Batu caves of Malaysia
A different Hindu shrine
A temple in a rock
272 steps to climb
During Thaipusam every year
Millions of pilgrims meet
A spectacular exhibition
Of Masochistic feats

49. Rubber

Natural rubber production
Malaysia was the chief
Now the largest producer
Of the protective sheaf
Johnnies, condoms, rubbers
Coming out of their ears
Home of the Durex headquarters
Five billion made a year

50. Muay Thai

In the beginning
So civilised and calm
Art of the sacred dance
No cause for alarm
Then the bell rings
Behind the wire fence
A frenzied crowd erupts
Let battle commence
Punches, kicks, elbow strikes
The highs and the lows
Only one rule to remember
'Anything goes'
Artful feints, lethal hits
A fight to place your bets
A crazed, electric atmosphere
You never will forget

51. Did the earth move for you?

An extended honeymoon
Passions still running high
We cuddled up for the evening
In a place they call Chiang Mai
Two lovers under the covers
I lent over, switched off the light
...I asked her in the morning
"Did the earth move for you last night?"
As usual she had no recollection
Her memory again did fail
She'd only slept through an earthquake
5.1 on the Richter scale

52. King

The Thais love their King
Sixty years at the top
World's longest reigning monarch
No signs that he will stop
Revered by his people
Like religion, both divine
Please don't insult either
You may end up serving time
Sea of yellow across a country
Royal emblem on everything
Like a heart upon a sleeve
Long live the King!

53. Shit happens

A parasite has befriended me
Is playing me for a fool
Sending me daily messages
Hidden in my stool
Not quite the travel bug
I had planned to catch
The antibiotics are struggling
Perhaps I'll light a match?
Oh no, I will not give up
It may get tired and take a nap
I have faith in the doctors
I know they'll 'cut the crap'
And that's just what they did
But they had to look inside
"Show yourself you slime ball"
There is no place to hide
There you are, we found you
With our microscopic lens
Enough of you controlling
When my shit happens!

54. School-tide

It was warm and the shops all open
My mind had trouble taking stock
Afternoon and people everywhere
A yuletide in Bangkok
It's just not what I'm used to
It should be cold and maybe snow
In old 'Blighty' deserted streets
A nation on 'go slow'
But what was most unnerving
On the pavement in our way
Was dodging all the school children
All this on Christmas Day

55. Slow boat

Thailand to Laos on the slow boat
Was an ordeal, not to repeat?
Crammed in like tinned sardines
Bags and people at your feet
Not much to eat, not much to do
On wooden planks you're sat
Occasionally someone jumps on board
To sell some barbecued rat!
It may take an age to get there
Hard going to say the least
But it's safer than the speedboats
And you'll get there in one piece

56. Angkor what?

Bas-reliefs
Sculpted stone
Many monuments
Never alone
Heritage hike
Walking boots
Temple ruins
Oozing roots
Historic site
Massive place
Balloon flight
Smiling face
Buddhist home
Spirit remain
Pilgrim magnet
Religious fame
World invited
Country's core
Cambodia's jewel
Amazing Angkor

57. Crown jewels

Angkor is their crown jewel
Cambodians hold it dear
Flying proudly on the flag
Upon their ciggies and their beer

58. Leap of faith

How does the traveller cross the road?
With difficulty it would seem
In Ho Chi Minh, Vietnam
Motorbikes you will dream
Questions you may ask yourself...
Will I live until I'm old?
Or make it to the other side?
The future is untold
Forget what you have learnt before
Forget the 'Green Cross Code'
Remember this survival tip
When you have to cross the road:
You must take a leap of faith
Your instincts must be ignored
Don't try to make a dash for it
Or curl up on the floor
Keep an eye on the traffic
Don't run, just have belief
Walk slowly as they steer around
That's it...feel the relief!

59. Play the game

Every thirty seconds
They hassle as they trade
Hello, cheap price, come look
Suits and shoes, all tailor made
So when in Rome, or Vietnam
Do as the sellers do
Play them at their own game
They won't have a clue
Where you from? How long you stay?
Ask, before they have the chance
You'll take them by surprise
You'll have them in a trance
They won't know what to do
They won't know what to say
By the time they've worked it out
You'll be off and on your way

60. Greasy Chopstick

Some places to eat in Asia
Are so dirty they make you sick
Just like our 'Greasy Spoon' at home
They have their 'Greasy Chopstick'

61. Splash act

Try to avoid the front row
As you may get a little wet
Theatre with a difference
A pool of water for a set
Add a splash of colour
A drop of music to set the scene
Soak up the atmosphere
Float into the Vietnam dream
Awash with legend and myth
With masters you cannot see
A fantasy world comes to life
The art of water puppetry

62. Tortured by the beast

So much of Asia's different
Then again the same, same
They all have one thing in common
But where to lay the blame?
Roaring out of speakers
A present from the East
Escaping from captivity
An uncontrollable beast
Scary and unpredictable
Oh! Please release me
A multiplying continent
Addicted to karaoke

63. Dirty laundry

In Britain we're so reserved
Business is done behind closed doors
The act of keeping up appearances
For the 'curtain twitching' neighbours
In Asia it's just the opposite
They don't care who's in the know
Air their laundry on the street
Gather round, enjoy the show
Shouting, fighting, hurling insults
Come close, pull up a pew
A liberating refreshing change
"Whose wife went off with who?"

64. Happy Valley

In Hong Kong is it OK?
To lose it all on one race
All your life's savings
Gone without a trace
How to explain the greed
To bet on a horse
Lost in the moment
At the race course
To justify the gamble
As you leave the house
"I'm off to give to the needy"
An excuse for the spouse
Is that why they call it 'Happy Valley'
Home of Angel and Sinner
As they donate loads to charity
...everyone's a winner?

65. Hong Kong wrong

Night becomes day
With a different sun
Reflecting modern life
Blurring into one
Flashing lights, neon signs
Advertising overload
Simply too much to take
Information implode
Universal balance lost
Hard to find your way
All meaning disappears
It can't be good Feng Shui?

66. Fragrant Harbour

What have they got in common
Blackpool, England and Hong Kong?
They have double-decker trams
Tacky lights and both do pong!

67. Stand out

Some people want to be noticed
To stand out from the crowd
A westerner in rural China
Will stand out 'clear and loud'
No matter what you wear
How you walk, talk or sing?
An undercover spy...
Would have trouble blending in
I kinda liked the interest
The blatant curiosity
The pointing, the staring, the intrigue
No concept of privacy
"Helloooo" they yell at you
"Laowai" ...the foreigner
Like an alien from outer space
You'll really cause a stir
But sometimes you need to escape
Some relief in the toilet will do?
No luck, the partitions are so low
Your neighbour can watch you poo!

68. Split pants

Like mini marshmallow people
But only a few years old
They waddle, stumble and wobble
All wrapped up from the cold
So cuddly and cute they look
Unfortunately, there's a catch
Each toddler has installed
A waste disposal hatch
On the street, the bus, no warning
They'll take you by surprise
Take aim, fire, bombs away
Try to avert your eyes

69. Travel wall

I scaled some of the Great Wall
And I'm proud to tell you so
As I was scared half to death
Because of my vertigo
My ordeal felt like an eternity
I was overcome with fear
I just wanted to shout out loud
"I'm a tourist, get me out of here!"
No turning back, no place to hide
Onwards and upwards the only way
I should have felt love in my heart
Not pain on Valentine's day
"Why am I doing this?"
I asked myself a million times
As I gripped harder and harder
The hands of my concubines
In the arms of two Chinese angels
Perhaps, who saved my life
Not how I imagined St Valentine's
Our first as husband and wife

70. The Chairman

The famous Mao, the Chairman
Modern China's architect
Arises daily from his freezer
Line up, pay your respects
They file up in their masses
Wait for their special view
It's the only time the Chinese
Can form an orderly queue
No joking around, no giggling
No talking, don't even cough
Try to forget the rumour
That his ear fell off!
A man who wanted to be cremated
And who always had his way
Ironically, is pickled forever
As for once they didn't obey
Like a Madame Tussaud's exhibit
Like wax, a face so smooth
In the heart of Beijing lies a corpse
That nobody dare remove

71. New Olympic event

If hacking and spitting were an Olympic event
The Chinese would surely win gold
They practice day and night
The young ones and the old
But when they receive their medal
Up there on the podium
They'd probably slip in a pool of phlegm
And fall down on their bum!

72. Quiet please!

I searched everywhere I could
Between the bikes in Beijing
Amongst the Terracotta Army
I couldn't find a thing
Up on the Great Wall
I went to take a look
Along the Yangtze river
...in the Peking duck
My efforts were in vain
In the noise I'd have to drown
In China they can't have a switch
To turn their volume down!

73. Law of the sod

A magical journey, it wasn't to be
On the Trans-Siberian Express
Trapped with a pain in the…
Whose lies did cause distress
An exercise in killing time
That's not all I wanted to kill
Days on end, losing track
Carry on, I lost the will
Had I sinned in a previous life?
I promised to try harder
Stuck in a sleeper carriage
With the devil in fake Prada
Travel 'chums' you can't always choose
It's all in the luck of the draw
The moral of the story is
I guess that's just sods law!

74. Rightful ruler

To utter his name was illegal
Of their hero they could but dream
Now his name is everywhere
Since the fall of the communist regime
Born into a noble blooded clan
That had fallen upon hard times
He rose to become the 'Rightful Ruler'
Avenging those who committed crimes
A Mongolian legend shrouded in mystery
His power reached far and wide
The 'Conqueror of the world'
It was wise to take his side
A nomad leader, always on the move
No known birthplace, no known address
No site left to commemorate the man
His name has lived on nonetheless
Ironically it's those who feared him most
Whose monument to him stands out
After all the Great Wall of China was built
To keep Genghis Khan and the Mongols out!

75. You can leave your hat on?

Never mind the nine million horses
They have almost as much headgear
About one hundred kinds of hats in Mongolia
Two for every week of the year
Men's, women's and children's
Religious, ornamental and state
Deciding which one to wear…
They are probably always late?
Take your hat off to them
Just don't put it on the ground
Exchange it or give it away
For bad luck you will have found

76. Red tape

We agonised for hours
Didn't know what to do
Stuck on the border to Russia
So much red tape to cut through
Do we or don't we?
What usually is the norm?
Declare the tune on our MP3
On our immigration form?
Almost cried ourselves a river
It had to be a mistake?
Don't smuggle any music in…
By Justin Timberlake!

77. Have faith

Be careful when using a phrasebook
I found this out to my regret
I pointed to the wrong word
A moment that's hard to forget
In a church in the middle of Russia
With a nun we couldn't understand
I pointed to 'atheist' not 'agnostic'
Ooops! The fires of hell I'd fanned
Horrified and shocked don't come close
To describe the look of her disgrace
Thought I'd sent her to heaven early
I hurriedly tried to save face
With a lot of smiles and many nods
We tried to communicate
And patiently listened to her sermon
As it started to get late
If we hadn't made our move
We would probably still be there
Let this be a warning to you
With your phrasebook do take care!

78. Grin and share it?

As a child my parents told me
When I was sulking like a prat
"When the wind changes
Your face will stay like that!"
I never believed it true
Until in Russia for a while
I came round to their suggestion
As no one seems to smile
Miserable, glum and moody
Like a sad circus clown
How do you say in Russian?
"Turn your frown upside down"

79. Final destination?

Circumnavigating the globe
Trains, planes, automobiles
Hasn't all been plain sailing?
Had our ups, had our squeals
Unforgettable coach journeys
Through many a beautiful place
But it's hard to enjoy the views
When your life flashes before your face
Speeding up the Mexican hills
Rallying round Malaysia's highlands
Praying to who will listen
No circulation in the hands
Stranded with 'crocs' in Australia
A bit worrying I must confess
Burst tyre in New Zealand
Train delays in the U.S.
Our only 'crash' of the trip
In China's capital Beijing
A 'write-off' at two miles per hour
A fuss over nothing
On our last flight back
As the skies were overcast
Welcome home from British Airways
They'd saved the best till last
The bumpiest landing of the lot
And no time to get jetlag
Not yet stepped onto UK soil
And they'd gone and lost our bag!

80. Travel Charades

Travelling without the local lingo
Is a bit like 'Give Us a Clue?'
Gesture with your hands and face
To get your message through
You might not get what you want
Sometimes if looks could kill?
It's not easy to be understood
But you'll always get the bill!

Final thoughts

I hope this collection of poems has made you smile, made you giggle, made you think, made you question and perhaps inspired you to think a little more about the world around you and what it has to offer. Has it given you a rhyming reason to travel the globe…or not? If it has please remember, wherever you go whether it be a thousand steps away or a thousand miles, take home with you memories and photographs but leave only footprints!

10% of the author's profits will be donated to environmental charities

Adapted from a Cree Indian Prophecy

Only after the last tree has been cut down
Only after the last river has been poisoned
Only after the last fish has been caught
Only after the last fossil fuel has been exhausted
Only after the last of the air has been polluted
Only after the last of the land has been sown
Only after the last ice cap has melted
Only then will we find out that money cannot be eaten
And the planet will finally be beaten

Street Art, USA

'Individually we are one drop, together we are an ocean'
- *Ryunosuke Satoro*

About the Author

I, Graham Relton, the author, now I like the sound of that. My strict English teacher at Secondary School was the trigger in my life…to turn my back on the literary world. In fact it took me almost five years to read a book for pleasure rather than necessity. And it took me a further seven years or so until I penned my first poem as an adult. A few Valentine's, Christmas and birthday poems later for family and friends and the habit stuck. It started out for fun and this is how it remains. During 2005 and 2006 I had a few poems published in compilation books and in March 2006 I stepped off the career ladder with my then girlfriend and now wife to circumnavigate the globe. I started writing poems in the first week of the trip in a hostel in the heart of Mexico City for pleasure and as a way of documenting the once in a lifetime adventure we had embarked on. I carried on writing up until the last leg of our epic journey on the Trans-Siberian Express across China and Mongolia to Russia. Echoing fellow Yorkshire man Ian McMillan and with a touch of Purple Ronnie thrown in my poetry is mainly tongue-in-cheek, however read between the lines and some serious issues are addressed. Around the World in 80 Poems is my first book and I hope it inspires, amuses and questions you the reader, giving you rhyming reasons to travel the globe…or not!

10% of the author's profits will be donated to environmental charities

Printed in the United Kingdom
by Lightning Source UK Ltd.
124665UK00002B/64-69/A